Poems a Plenty

Poems a Plenty

Volume 1

By Tura Covill

RESOURCE *Publications* • Eugene, Oregon

POEMS A PLENTY
Volume 1

Copyright © 2019 Tura Covill. All rights reserved. Except for brief quotations in critical publications or reviews, no part of this book may be reproduced in any manner without prior written permission from the publisher. Write: Permissions, Wipf and Stock Publishers, 199 W. 8th Ave., Suite 3, Eugene, OR 97401.

Resource Publications
An Imprint of Wipf and Stock Publishers
199 W. 8th Ave., Suite 3
Eugene, OR 97401

www.wipfandstock.com

PAPERBACK ISBN: 978-1-7252-5755-9
HARDCOVER ISBN: 978-1-7252-5756-6
EBOOK ISBN: 978-1-7252-5757-3

Manufactured in the U.S.A. 12/02/19

Author Tura Covill, Age 100

CONTENTS

Jesus Died upon the Cross | 1
Walk With Jesus | 2
You Ask so Very Little | 3
Say Your Prayers | 4
God Knows | 5
Valuable Advice | 6
A Crown of Glory | 7
What Would You Do? | 8
By God's Guidance | 9
Powerful Jesus | 10
Everyone Jesus Sees | 11
You Won't Be Turned Away | 12
Don't Ever Fear | 13
Mansions and Dreams | 14
Results from Sin | 15
No Pay | 16
Disaster Strikes | 17
So True, So True | 18
Beautiful Creation | 19
Thank You Lord | 20
A Samaritan Stopped By | 21
Glorify Jesus | 22
Recipe for Life | 23
A Home in Heaven | 24

Record Book | 25
A Book Called "Truth" | 26
Daniel in the Lion's Den | 27
Lord Lead Me On | 28
Temptation of Christ | 29
There is a Time | 30
Bible Stands for Truth | 31
Dear Lord | 32
He Can Read Your Mind | 33
Holding Habits | 34
Fight the Battle | 35
Disappointed Jesus | 36
Before I Gave My Heart to God | 37
Power of Love | 38
Noah Built an Ark | 39
School of Jesus | 40
God Can | 41
Garden of Eden | 42
Our Prayers | 43
Now Is the Time | 44
Now Listen to Jesus | 45
On That Rugged Cross | 46
Reaching Up | 47

JESUS DIED UPON THE CROSS

Jesus died upon the cross
And He died for you and me
He shed His blood; He suffered
With so much pain and agony.
    Nails were driven in His hands,
    And they were also in His feet.
    Such a cruel act had taken place,
    And they wanted it complete.
Lord Jesus suffered for our sins
With the thorns put on His head,
With blood dripping on His face
Now here's what the Saviour said,
    "Father forgive them for
    They know not what they do."
    So many stood there watching
    The whole procedure through.
They beat Him, and mocked Him,
And pierced Him as they frowned.
Saying, "If you're the Son of God,
Why don't you come on down?"
    Jesus could have called His angels,
    But He died while suffering there.
    To save us from the sins we do.
    No better love that can compare.

By Tura (Vandervoort) Covill
Luke 23:34; Matt. 27:27–48

WALK WITH JESUS

Take a little walk with Jesus
As He takes you by the hand;
He will tell you all about
His great and promised land.

Take a little walk with Jesus
While your future lies ahead.
Always stay with Him forever,
And spiritually you'll be led.

Take a little walk with Jesus
While journeying along the way.
Never turn your back on Jesus,
But walk with Him each day.

By Tura (Vandervoort) Covill
John 14:16; Psalms 32:8

YOU ASK SO VERY LITTLE

Oh how powerful you are Lord
To create so many things.
All those flowers and trees,
Those that happiness brings.
    Great power of your majesty,
    The greatness of your love.
    Thinking of us here below
    When YOU have so much above.
The splendor of your heavens.
All the host of angels there
Still you have thought of us
With your tender love, you care.
    Your crown and precious jewels
    That is yours in heaven above.
    You offered them to us to have
    With a generous amount of love.
You have so much to offer us
With your pure heart of concern,
And you ask so very little Lord.
What can we give you in return?

By Tura (Vandervoort) Covill
John 14:21; 1 Timothy 6:14

SAY YOUR PRAYERS

If you are sad and have no hope;
Trials of life you cannot cope.
You have a feeling no one cares,
Talk to Jesus, say your prayers.

You wonder why it happened to you.
Someday you'll know about it too.
God will explain all your despair,
Right now kneel, say your prayer.

If you don't trust God or believe
Day after day you sit and grieve.
Prayers are answered everywhere.
You'll be blessed say your prayers.

Don't blame God what happens to you
Blame Satan he is right there too.
Satan hates because he doesn't care,
But Jesus loves, so say your prayers.

By Tura (Vandervoort) Covill
1 John 3:22; Hosea 10:12

GOD KNOWS

God knows
How many tears we shed
   He knows
How many prayers we said
   God knows.

   God knows
The life that we live
   He knows
The comfort that He gives
   God knows.

   God knows
Our days of loneliness
   He knows
Our thoughts we have, oh yes
   God knows.

By Tura (Vandervoort) Covill
Luke 8:17; Jer. 23:24

VALUABLE ADVICE

Leave all your troubles to Jesus
Because He knows just what to do.
Be sure and trust in Him always
As He hears every word from you.

Just ask Him what you want to;
He will listen to what you say.
This is the way to communicate
When you go to Jesus and pray.

Your turn will soon be coming
When ever you will be blessed.
So leave all troubles to Jesus;
He will take care of the rest.

By Tura (Vandervoort) Covill
Isaiah 41:13; Proverbs 3:6

A CROWN OF GLORY

A crown of immortal glory
Will be placed upon our head.
With riches of eternal life
That is what the Bible said.

Honors that are everlasting
Are given to us with care.
As Jesus is the almighty
Who is always good and fair.

A crown of greatest splendor
We will wear in Jesus' name.
They are made for everyone,
But they will not be the same.

And the crown is ours forever,
Covered with jewels so rare,
A treasure especially for us
Is waiting in heaven there.

By Tura (Vandervoort) Covill
Rev. 3:11; Rev. 2:10

WHAT WOULD YOU DO?

If Jesus knocked upon your door
As He decided to visit with you,
And you were smoking a cigarette,
Now, really what would you do?

If He came while you were drunk,
And He wanted to talk with you.
Just what excuse would you make?
Having drinks in plain view?

If Jesus walked into your house,
And He bowed His head in prayer,
Praying for you to His Father,
Would you then thank Him there?

Don't try to hide your thoughts,
And think Jesus will not know.
If He'd ask you to follow Him,
Would you tell Him you would go?

Jesus stands outside your door.
He is knocking, and knows your sin.
Would you welcome Jesus Christ,
And be happy that He came on in?

By Tura (Vandervoort) Covill
Matthew 24:14; Mark 13:37

BY GOD'S GUIDANCE

How can the tree hold on to its leaves
Whenever the wind blows hard and long?
How can the birds fly up in the air
When the rain comes down so strong?
    BY GOD'S GUIDANCE
When the strong wind shakes the trees,
Then what keeps the birds in the nest?
It is all by power and faith in God,
Because it comes from the very best.
    BY GOD'S GUIDANCE
How can the mountains stay at its peak
When loaded with much snow on the top?
How can the rivers keep on flowing.
Every day and night and never stop?
    BY GOD'S GUIDANCE
How can flowers bloom on this earth,
To produce beauty in deserts, and yet,
How can creatures survive in the wild
When they cannot find any food to get?
    BY GOD'S GUIDANCE
How can this old world stand up at all
With so much evil pulling it down?
And how can everyone do anything right
With Satan and his angels around?
    BY GOD'S GUIDANCE

By Tura (Vandervoort) Covill
Psalms 32:8; Isaiah 41:10

POWERFUL JESUS

Jesus took five loaves of bread;
He then took two little fishes;
Jesus fed five thousand people.
He fulfilled all their wishes.
    Matthew 14:17–21
Then, Jesus also raised the dead:
He raised them from the grave.
Powerful Jesus can do it again,
And call His saints forth to save.
    2 Samuel 2:6
Jesus walked across the water;
With every step He did not sink.
So many people had watched Him
Right from that water's brink.
    Matthew 14:24–31
A touch on the hills from Jesus
Will cause the smoke to descend.
You better believe in His power
Because Jesus' power has no end.
    Psalms 104:32
Jesus has healed so many people,
By His word and even His touch,
Because He has the most power;
Of Course Jesus can do so much.
    Matthew 8:13

By Tura (Vandervoort) Covill

EVERYONE, JESUS SEES

He sees each tear that's in the eye.
He sees the hours and days go by.
He sees the people not doing right.
He sees all day; He sees all night.

He sees the meek; He sees the brave.
He sees lives He suffered to save.
He sees the nations falling apart.
He sees inside of everyone's heart.

He sees the pride that seems to last.
He sees the warnings that are passed.
He sees every sin that we do each day.
He sees His heartache here to stay.

He sees His law here printed in books.
He sees all secrets, He always looks.
He sees the large; He sees the small.
He sees everything - Jesus sees us all.

By Tura (Vandervoort) Covill
Mark 4:22; Matthew 5:14

YOU WON'T BE TURNED AWAY

Knock on the door of Jesus, now.
He'll welcome you inside to stay,
And offer you a hand of assurance.
He will always show you the way.
To that way of life and security
Where you will be safe there inside.
So knock on the door of Jesus now,
And with Jesus you can always abide.

YOU WON'T BE TURNED AWAY.

Knock on His door anytime my friend.
He will bless and comfort you too.
Tell Him your troubles—He'll listen.
He will gladly hear you on through.
Just stay as long as you want to stay.
There is no hurry to rush anymore.
Set by His side at His table there.
Be ready to always knock on His door.

YOU WON'T BE TURNED AWAY.

By Tura (Vandervoort) Covill
Rev. 3:20; Matthew 7:7

DON'T EVER FEAR

If your days are not so perfect,
Because you have a load of care.
All worries seem to stay around
Don't fear, the Lord is there.

He will always bring you comfort,
And I know that He loves you so.
Never fear, He is there with you,
And from you He will never go.

Now put your burdens at His feet;
Then you thank Him in your way.
He will make your life much better
But with much happiness every day.

With a prayer a constant longing;
And with dear Jesus in your mind.
A friend, a pal, a love forever
With Jesus I know you will find.

By Tura (Vandervoort) Covill
Psalms 9:9; Matthew 5:48

MANSIONS AND DREAMS

I dream of that mansion
Way up there in the sky.
I dream of the pathway
That leads up so high.

I know that God hears me
While I say my prayers.
He sees me from heaven,
And I know that He cares.

So I want to be with Him
In that mansion so high.
Jesus says He will come
To take us up in the sky.

This world is so wicked
It's a shame to be in it.
With corruption and sins.
It's the same every minute.

By Tura (Vandervoort) Covill
Matt. 7:21; 1 Thess. 4:17

RESULTS FROM SIN

Satan took the world away from Jesus.
Earth is corrupt and full of diseases,
And the air is clogged from impurities
While sin goes on and will never cease.

Flowers don't live long until they die,
Wilting away from the pollution supply.
The earth is so full of evil so thick.
No wonder people all go around sick.

Trees are molded, lined with diseases.
Satan takes over, doing as he pleases.
Killing is done by a great multitude
Because of Satan, he'll always intrude.

The water is not pure as it should be.
The world rots away, we plainly see.
Disaster, destruction is Satan's joy,
He sends temptation like a decoy.

By Tura (Vandervoort) Covill
Revelation 12:9

NO PAY

The healing that Jesus does
Is with love in His own way
No matter who the sick are
He healed them without pay.

He healed the man with palsy,
And cured the withered hand.
He healed the epileptic boy
All done with His command.

But no money did He ask for
Didn't charge a single cent.
From all the ones He healed
Each one went away content.

They all had faith in Jesus
The blind who could not see,
Crippled ones and deaf ones,
He healed them all for free.

He is the doctor of the world,
And is near as a prayer away.
He will take us by the hand.
With Him we can always pray.

By Tura (Vandervoort) Covill
Matthew 15:30; James 5:15

DISASTER STRIKES

There was a crash heard far and wide.
Screaming, suffering ones who've died.
So disaster played its leading part.
It often strikes and stops a heart.

So many people are killed each day
From careless drivers going each way.
With drunken drivers behind the wheel
So disaster strikes, this is so real.

God sees all this, and we wonder why?
If God loves us all, why did they die?
Jesus loves us all the Bible has told,
But sin is something He'll not uphold.

Jesus sent the Bible, but not the car.
He did not send liquor to us, by far.
So don't blame Jesus for worldly sin.
He had no intentions of entering in.

God heals, saves, loves and will bring.
Love to all if we do the right thing.
Who causes disaster? God's not to blame.
Disaster strikes, because sin overcame.

By Tura (Vandervoort) Covill

SO TRUE, SO TRUE

The world has rejected God's mercy,
And despised His love and His law.
The wicked ones will pass probation,
And the Spirit of God will withdraw.

No silver or gold will save them.
That day of wrath means trouble.
The heavens and earth will shake
Punishment then will come double.

Jesus has warned us so many times
That the time of the end is near.
But the world just will not listen
The Lord, they don't seem to fear.

Soon an angel will return from earth
Telling Jesus His people are sealed,
And the final test has been brought
So many sinners here will not yield.

By Tura (Vandervoort) Covill
Zephaniah 2:3; Zephaniah 1:18

BEAUTIFUL CREATION

God made every tree and formed them so.
Planned each leaf the way they must go.
He made every flower and each tiny seed.
He nourished them all with love indeed.

He made the sun and the moon up high,
And even the stars we see in the sky.
He made the oceans and rivers so wide.
Formed each wave, controls each tide.

He made all creatures on earth to roam.
Put two of a kind in pairs of its own.
God made grass green, and the sky blue
All over the world all the way through.

God made everything you better believe.
Prepared it for who? It was Adam and Eve.
Then we were born later to fill the earth.
Increasing life more from nature's birth.

The Lord looks down with a broken heart.
To see the people pulling His world apart.
Although He is sad, He does love everyone.
Beautiful creation, He thought well done.

By Tura (Vandervoort) Covill
Ecclesiastes 3:11; John 1:3

THANK YOU LORD

Thank you for our health Lord,
And the shelter over our head.
Thank you for prayers answered,
And the example you have led.

Thank you for food and clothes,
And your guidance so very true.
Thank you for a home in heaven
That you prepared for us too.

Thank you for so many things
That you have given us today.
Thank you for your tender love
That is with us here to stay.

By Tura (Vandervoort) Covill
1 Chron. 16:34; 1 Chron. 23:30

A SAMARITAN STOPPED BY

A certain man went from Jerusalem to Jericho;
And there were thieves which robbed him; so,
They wounded him and they left him half dead.
This story is true. In the Bible it is said.
    The traveler went through a rocky ravine there;
    Found the man bruised and blood was everywhere.
    But he turned around and he left the man lay;
    And he never came back the rest of the day.
Then a Levite appeared, and he stopped to see.
The poor old man was suffering so pitifully.
The Levite wandered just what all he could do;
So, then, he left the poor man lying there too.
    Then along came a Samaritan down the same way;
    And he saw the man who was wounded as he lay.
    With gentle kindness he helped as he should.
    He bound up his wounds and did what he could;
Then, he picked him up and put him on his horse;
So he could travel on the regular same course.
He took him to an inn and took care of him;
Gave the innkeeper money and then left again.

By Tura (Vandervoort) Covill
John 15:17; Rom. 12:21; Luke 10:30–35

GLORIFY JESUS

Will you come when the Master calls?
Or will you linger until too late?
Would you let Him lead your life?
Would you come, or would you wait?

Don't be afraid to walk with Him
And just trust Jesus, in every way.
Will you follow His path of perfection
And put your mind at ease each day?

Don't let cares of life drag you down,
But glorify Jesus in your life.
Notice the time goes by much faster
Away from your worry and strife.

By Tura (Vandervoort) Covill
1 Peter 4:16; Matt. 5:16; 1 Cor. 6:20

RECIPE FOR LIFE

Follow this recipe for life
As it is an easy one to make.
It's something anyone can do,
And all for happiness sake.

Take one cup of Christianity,
Mixed with one cup of love.
Then strain out all the sins
That Satan has mixed thereof.

Now, add some pleasant wishes.
A cup of good thought seeds.
A teaspoon full of respect,
And concern for all in need.

Stir in a lot of faith in God,
And handle this all with care;
And add a cup full of devotion.
Your recipe for life is there.

By Tura (Vandervoort) Covill
John 6:35; Matthew 5:6

A HOME IN HEAVEN

All the finest things in life
That just anyone can own
It is living with our Saviour
There in His heavenly home.

We would never need for money,
Or ever need to go to a store.
We would not want for anything,
Or ever have to fight a war.

We would never once get tired,
Or have any pain or sorrow.
We would never have a worry
About the coming of tomorrow.

We would never have to die;
No more killing or any tears.
We would never count our days,
Or live in dreadful fears.

A home with the Lord in heaven.
There is nothing to compare.
All that Jesus promised for us
Is waiting in heaven there.

By Tura (Vandervoort) Covill
Isa. 25:8; Luke 22:29, 30

RECORD BOOK

When our life is over, and
Jesus comes to earth again,
We must have a pure heart
From all this earthly sin.

Whether we are good or bad,
It is recorded in God's book.
When time of judgement comes
God will open it and look.

Then when this book is opened,
We are judged from all we do;
So let our names be spotless
Whenever our life is through.

By Tura (Vandervoort) Covill
Rev. 3:3; Proverbs 7:2, 3

A BOOK CALLED "TRUTH"

If you want to know the truth,
Now the truth is in the book.
All you have to do my friend
Is to stop and take a look.

The book is called the Bible.
And it has the facts for you.
Compare those scriptures here,
Then you will find it's true.

You wonder where the truth is,
And which way you should go.
So take a little time and read;
And then the truth you'll know.

If one really wants to learn it,
From the old, or to the youth,
The past, the present, or future,
Just read the book called "Truth".

By Tura (Vandervoort) Covill
2 Timothy 1:13; Proverbs 4:5

DANIEL IN THE LION'S DEN

Daniel was safer in the lion's den
Than he would have been in the court.
Because he kept very close to Jesus,
And to Him everything he'd report.
   The king really didn't hate Daniel,
   But he had him throwed into the den.
   Down there with the hungry lions
   Surrounding him again, and again.
So much faith Daniel had in God
As the snarling beasts stood nearby.
Then he kneeled to pray to Jesus
For the Lord would not let him die.
   Now the king who put him in there
   Came to see if He was dead.
   But he found Daniel alive and well,
   And the lion's stood around instead.
That made the king a believer too;
He could see that God could save.
They took Daniel out of the den,
And thought He was very brave.
   So all the men who accused Him
   Were cast there in the lion's den.
   As well as the wives and children;
   The lions had the mastery of them.

By Tura (Vandervoort) Covill
Luke 12:2–12; Dan. 12:10; Dan. 6:10–28

LORD LEAD ME ON

Lord please lead me on.
Where you want me to go,
And just place my mind
On things I should know.

Lead me, I'll follow you,
And I'll promise to stay.
And always walk with you
While I live, day by day.

Please lead me straight,
Like a shepherd does trod,
To that path of eternity
Straight up to you God.

Just show me the way Lord,
To that perfect delight,
I'll always be with you
Doing everything right.

By Tura (Vandervoort) Covill
2 Chronicles 15:7; Psalms 94:14

TEMPTATION OF CHRIST

Satan tried to tempt our Saviour.
He promised the world at His feet,
But Jesus says, "Get thee hence",
And He said it quite complete.

Satan tried to offer Him power
With all glory there untold.
If Jesus would only worship him,
And forever his words to unfold.

Satan said, "Turn a stone to bread"
So the hungry Saviour could eat,
"Man cannot live by bread alone",
Those words our God did repeat.

Alright if you're the Son of God
Then cast yourself down below,
Then call your angels to rescue
If you are God's Son, you know.

Now get thee behind me Satan
To tempt me, you cannot succeed.
Just go away and leave me alone.
It is only My Father I need.

By Tura (Vandervoort) Covill
Matt. 16:41; Luke 4:1–15

THERE IS A TIME

There's a time to be born.
There is a time to die.
There's a time to smile.
There is a time to cry.

There's a time to say "yes"
There's a time to say "no".
There is a time to stop.
There is a time to go.

There's a time to be quiet.
There is a time to talk.
There is a time to run.
There is a time to walk.

There's a time to seek God.
There is a time to pray.
There is a time right now.
There is a time today.

By Tura (Vandervoort) Covill
Eccl. 3:1–8; 2 Pet. 3:8

BIBLE STANDS FOR TRUTH

If the Bible says one thing,
So, then should we do another
By doing just what we please;
Then teach it to our brother?

Really, that does contradict
The things that Jesus told.
He ordered the Bible written
Like treasures of pure gold.

God's words are so important
He preached to all, and yet
Not wanting His words changed.
Satan tries to make us forget.

Holy Bible stands for truth.
To those who reads its pages.
Let's not change God's Bible
Years ago, down through ages.

By Tura (Vandervoort) Covill
Psalms 12:6; John 14:21

DEAR LORD

Dear Lord you are precious,
   And the Bible is too.
Because we get the message
   Right directly from you.

You have saved us from sin
   With love and thought.
All the love that you have,
   And what all you taught.

Now I read in Your Bible
   As I read page to page.
That your love is forever,
   No matter what age.

So dear Lord I thank you
   As I kneel and pray.
I hope I am worthy Lord
   To be with you some day.

By Tura (Vandervoort) Covill
Isa. 40:8; Psalms 107:43

HE CAN READ YOUR MIND

The Lord is always with you,
And love with Him you'll find.
Jesus knows your every thought
Because He can read your mind.

So you cannot get away from Him.
There's no place for you to hide.
You're like a light upon a hill.
You can be seen from every side.

He can see your every move here.
Every thought you have He'll find.
He knows you better that you do
Because Jesus can read your mind.

By Tura (Vandervoort) Covill
Jeremiah 23:24; Luke 8:17

HOLDING HABITS

Are you nervous, and do you fret?
Why do you smoke that cigarette?
It ruins life like a sin or curse.
Smoking cigarettes makes life worse.

Are you confused, mind not thinking?
Then why should you keep on drinking,
Please Go to Jesus instead my friend
Surely you'll feel better in the end

Now are you hooked, without any hope;
Your nerves tight from using dope?
You will be more miserable my friend.
Why add troubles, bring it to an end?

Do you hold bad habits in your life:
Fighting, hating, constant strife?
It doesn't help, it is all in vain.
You are traveling in the wrong lane.

It's Satan's tricks, you cannot win.
If you hold the habits, it is a sin.
Ask Jesus for help, he understands
He will help you, obey His commands.

By Tura (Vandervoort) Covill
Romans 6:12; Isaiah 5:20

FIGHT THE BATTLE

God tries to warn each one of us
To avoid all of the devil's ways.
And our life is what we make it
While we live from day to day.

But Satan tempts in many ways,
And he tries to turn our head.
He sets and thinks of ideas
From the ones we have instead.

Our battle is fighting Satan,
And with God's help we will win
If we obey what Jesus tells us,
We will get protection from Him.

Take the name of Jesus with you,
Then you present it, every day.
It will help you fight the battle,
And it will keep the devil away.

By Tura (Vandervoort) Covill
James 1:14; Ephesians 6:10, 11

DISAPPOINTED JESUS

I have called, and you refused me.
I held out my hands for you to come.
But I saw you turn your head away,
And believe me that hurt me some.

If you don't need me I'll not bother.
I see you suffer heartaches and pain.
Why separate yourselves from me now.
What Satan offers is nothing to gain.

So think of the things I have offered.
Now if you follow my way and believe.
There's nothing to me impossible to do.
Please trust me, and do not grieve.

I have sent many teachers to teach you,
And there are many books you can read.
A very good life that I've offered you.
You can just call on me when in need.

By Tura (Vandervoort) Covill
Isaiah 65:2; Isaiah 66:4

BEFORE I GAVE MY HEART TO GOD

Before I gave my heart to God
I had missed so many things.
Flowers trees, such blessings:
Like little birds that sings.

I never saw the grass so green,
But I knew that it was there.
I never saw the forming clouds,
Or the sun so bright and fair.

I saw the fruit was on the trees
And growing with great care.
But I never gave it any thought
That the Lord had put it there.

But since I gave my heart to God,
Now I can see most everything.
The creation of all His power.
He's our Lord, our eternal King.

By Tura (Vandervoort) Covill
Genesis 1:11; Eccles. 3:11

POWER OF LOVE

A child was born in a manger bed.
A lowly place for His little head.
King of kings, a prince on earth.
Born to Mary as a special birth.

He was named Jesus, a mighty power.
As excitement grew within the hour.
Many people came from miles around
To see the babe, where to be found.

Following a star they were led
To a power lying in a manger bed.
Jesus grew to be a kind loving lad
A heart of love is what He had.

Obedience was what Jesus learned.
Obeying His parents was His concern.
So much thoughtfulness He had done.
To give love to the forgotten one.

Still today He's a wonderful Man
With His power, He takes His stand.
Doing good to others; not for fame.
Still today His love is the same.

By Tura (Vandervoort) Covill
Matthew 2:11; Luke 2:11–16

NOAH BUILT AN ARK

God had told Noah to build a large ark
It was on a sunny day, it was not dark.
Of course Noah always did as He was told,
But Noah at this time was 600 years old.
   So Noah and his family started right in.
   To Follow God's instructions and to begin.
   They all labored long and so very hard.
   And measured each board by foot and yard.
But Noah couldn't figure why this must be.
There had not been any rain in that century.
So Noah was ridiculed by the people around
He was building a ship upon a high ground.
   But Noah had great faith in the Lord always.
   He knew to obey God all the rest of his days.
   People made fun, and they would not believe
   Until the rain came, and then Noah did leave.
Noah and his family were safe there inside.
Riding along with the water deep and wide.
For forty days and nights the rain did fall.
Unbelievers were left, God drowned them all.
   When the flood ended Noah released a dove,
   To let him know if it's safe in God's love.
   Noah and his family lived on the dry land
   With creatures he saved with God's command.

By Tura (Vandervoort) Covill
Genesis 8:1–22; Genesis 7:1–24

SCHOOL OF JESUS

We are like school children.
We must learn to do our best.
To study hard and read a lot.
The Lord will teach the rest.

The Holy Bible we should read,
About how this earth was made
As our characters are recorded,
So to get our separate grades.

If our grades are not correct,
Jesus marks off all our errors
So we must pay more attention
To our Jesus Christ who cares.

Our grades must be to a standard.
Jesus will help us with our test
Then graduate us up into heaven
Where we can find peace and rest.

By Tura (Vandervoort) Covill
John 8:47; Deuteronomy 12:32

GOD CAN

Can you stop it from raining,
And can you put out the sun?
Can you feed every wild bird,
And not to forget even one?
   GOD CAN
Then can you make summer heat,
Or bring the winter weather?
Can you stop the raging winds,
And keep them all together?
   GOD CAN
Can you guide each footstep?
Can you answer each prayer?
Can you send out a rainbow,
And hang stars way up there?
   GOD CAN
Can you form all the clouds?
Can you make them disappear?
Can you tend to each detail
On this sinful world here?
   GOD CAN

By Tura (Vandervoort) Covill
Matt. 19:26; Jer. 32:27

GARDEN OF EDEN

God created a beautiful garden,
With flowers, grass, and trees,
And He blessed it with His love,
Planned with greatest of ease.

The Garden of Eden so beautiful
Perfected as plain as could be
A miracle method of generosity
But only the one forbidden tree.

The tree of knowledge standing
That no one must ever touch
But Satan said it was alright.
Eve's temptation was too much.

Eve took the fruit from off it;
Then she tasted it right there;
Then told Adam to do the same,
And they became a sinful pair.

By Tura (Vandervoort) Covill
Gen. 3:1–20; Rev. 20:2

OUR PRAYERS

Just why don't we get an answer
When our prayers go to the Lord?
Our life may be filled with hate
Which is Satan's dangerous sword.

How could it be that we do not
Have the patience that we should?
Could our mind be full of nonsense,
And we forget what is really good?

Just why don't we get an answer
From our prayer so often said?
Our faith may be rather lacking
While we are hanging by a thread.

There are many people saying,
"If all prayers are only heard
There would be much less sorrow
By following our Saviour's word".

By Tura (Vandervoort) Covill
John 15:7; John 8:47

NOW IS THE TIME

Now is the time to give warning
To the inhabitants near and far
That Jesus will come so suddenly
He will catch us just as we are.

There will be no time to prepare;
So we better be ready right now
Christ is in charge of this world,
And all sins Jesus will not allow.

Warnings from Christ we must fear
As the former things come to pass.
So warn all those who will listen.
Sinners will burn like the grass.

As Jesus will cleanse the earth,
And get rid of all of the sin.
Now is the time to give warning;
Right now is the time to begin.

By Tura (Vandervoort) Covill
Col. 1:28; Ezekiel 3:17

NOW LISTEN TO JESUS

Now hear the truthful words
That Jesus has here to say.
All promises that He gives
It's for you and me today.

Jesus knows our every move.
And He is up in heaven above.
He watches with tender care
While sending down His love.

The Bible has the commandments
God's rules that we have read.
He tells us what we must do;
With His Spirit we are fed.

With our Bible and the Lord
Jesus will lead us every day.
We don't need any more in life.
He'll show us the perfect way.

By Tura (Vandervoort) Covill
Luke 24:44; Joshua 1:8

ON THAT RUGGED CROSS

On the cross He sealed my pardon.
He paid the debt, He made me free.
No one here that is under heaven
Will ever mean as much to me.

Jesus is my very life, my all.
He is the way that I must live.
I cannot do enough for Jesus
For all blessings He does give.

So when I bow my head in prayer,
And sincerely to Jesus I'll pray,
I always have faith He'll answer
As He does many times each day.

On that old cross He died for me,
But now He is alive, and is well.
And willing to help us if we obey,
The Bible has more it can tell.

By Tura (Vandervoort) Covill
Rev. 14:12; Psalms 27:14

REACHING UP

You're reaching up to Jesus
He is reaching down to you.
He loves you very, very much
And hopes you love Him too.

Jesus wants you to obey Him.
He will reach for you and bless.
The touch of the Master's hand
Can bring you much happiness.

While you reach toward heaven.
You must love Him oh so true.
Jesus is your blessed Saviour
And He's reaching down to you".

By Tura (Vandervoort) Covill
Nahum 1:7 ; Prov. 3:1–13

www.ingramcontent.com/pod-product-compliance
Lightning Source LLC
Chambersburg PA
CBHW072037060426
42449CB00010BA/2316